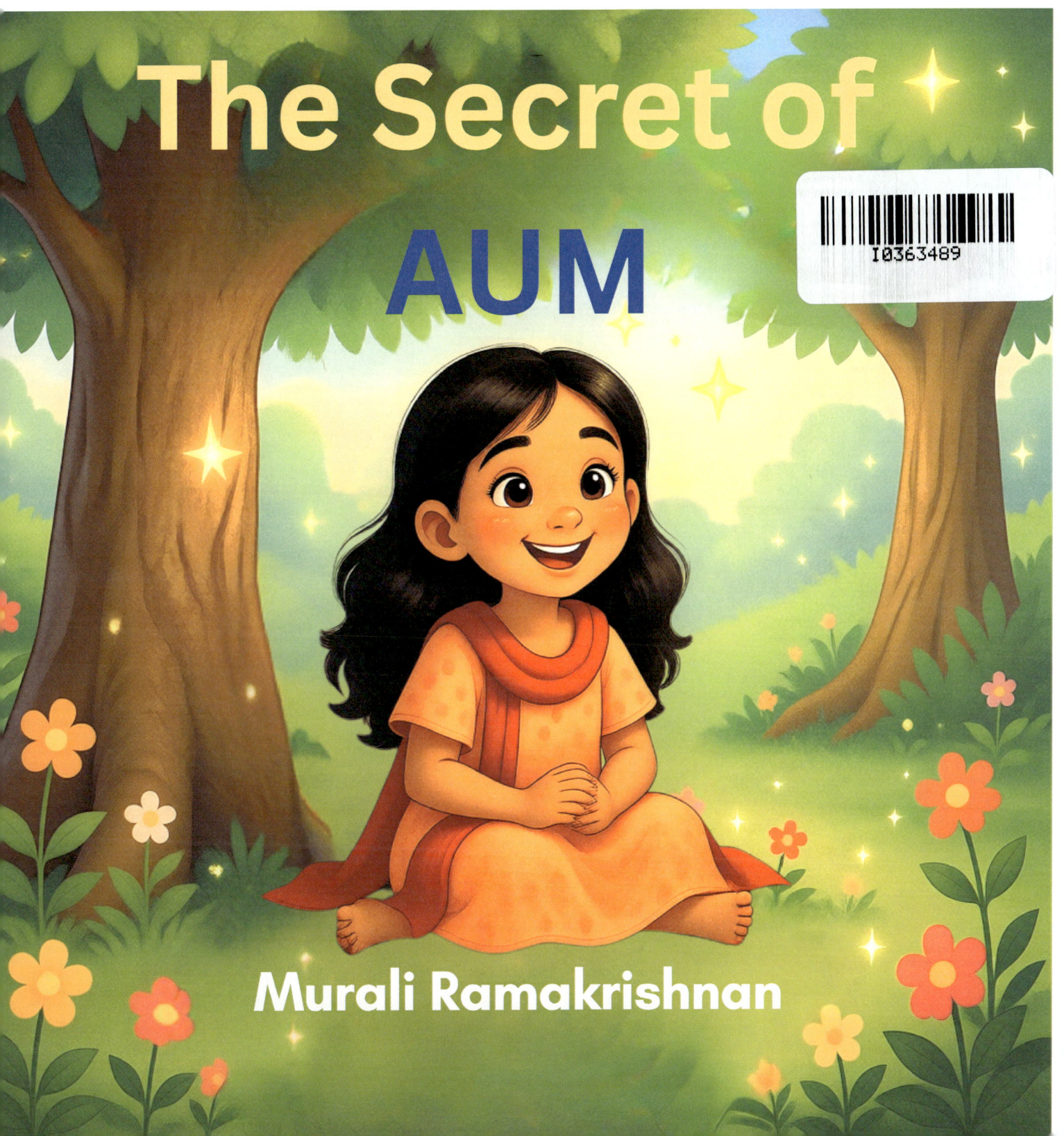

The Secret of AUM
Written by Murali Ramakrishnan

© 2025 Murali Ramakrishnan
All rights reserved.

AI Generated Illustrations

No part of this book may be copied or reproduced in any form without permission from the author or publisher.

Published by Sunadham Publishing
First Edition, 2025

This book belongs to

Morning sunlight filled the garden with gold. Nisha skipped between the plants until one flower caught her eye — bright pink, soft, and shining like a tiny sun.

"Hello, beautiful!" she said, bending close. The flower seemed to smile back.

The next morning, Nisha ran to see her friend again.

"Oh no!" she gasped. The petals had turned brown and drooped. The flower looked tired and dull.

Nisha's heart felt heavy. "Why did you have to change?" she whispered.

Just then, she heard a gentle laugh. Looking up, Nisha saw the old tree shaking its leaves as if amused

"What are you laughing at?" she asked crossly.
The tree's deep voice rumbled kindly. "You look sad, little one. Has your flower changed?"

"Yes," said Nisha, pouting. "It was so pretty yesterday!"

The tree chuckled "Look closely. There are new flowers blooming right beside it."

Nisha turned – three new blossoms had opened!

The tree said, "Here's a challenge for you: can you find something that never changes?"

Nisha's eyes lit up. "I'll try!"

All day Nisha searched Trees grew, clouds moved, even people changed Then she spotted a huge rock by the stream.
"You!" she said "You must never change."

To her surprise, the rock rumbled, "I was once a mountain, worn down by wind and rain. Someday I'll become sand"
Nisha sighed "So even you change."

That night, Nisha looked up at the stars. "Oh bright ones," she called softly, "are you forever the same?"

The stars twinkled and replied, "Not really, dear Nisha. Some of us faded long ago. The light you see began its journey when we were alive."

Nisha's brow furrowed "Everything changes!

She lay in bed, thinking hard. The flower, the rock, even the stars – all changing!
The moonlight fell across her blanket as she wondered, "Is there anything that stays the same?"
Sleep came quietly, wrapping her in silver dream

Next morning she told the tree, "I looked everywhere, but everything changes."

The tree smiled gently. "That's all right. Tonight, go to sleep and tell me about your dream tomorrow. Perhaps your answer hides there."

That night, Nisha dreamt she was driving her father's car – only it could fly!

She soared past colourful stars and silver clouds.

"Hi Nisha!" one star called "I spoke to you yesterday!"

Another star winked "Don't forget your homework!"

Nisha gasped "Oh no, I forgot!" She suddenly woke up, relieved "Phew! I finished it yesterday!"

The next day, Nisha told the tree her funny dream.

"In your dream," asked the tree, "did you know you were dreaming?"

Nisha shook her head. "No. It felt completely real."

The tree's leaves rustled softly. "Good. Tonight, eat early and rest. Tell me tomorrow what happens."

That evening, Nisha ate her dinner quietly and went to bed early.
No dreams came — only deep, peaceful sleep, like floating in gentle darkness.
When she awoke, her mind felt fresh, her heart calm.

"Tree," she said next morning, "I don't remember any dreams. I just slept."

"Do you remember anything at all?" asked the tree.

"No," said Nisha, "but I know I slept well."

The tree said "Interesting. You did not know anything, except one thing. That you slept well. That means something inside you watched you while you were sleeping"

The Tree continued softly, "The part of you that sees the flower, dreams of flying, and knows you slept — is it always there?"

Nisha thought for a moment. "Yes, you're right. There's something inside me that watches all these three worlds."

The Tree nodded. "Yes, that same thing watches everything. But remember — it only watches. It never changes."

Nisha thought for a moment. "What about you, Tree? Is there something inside you that watches too?"

The Tree paused, its leaves shimmering in the light. "Shall I tell you a secret?"

Nisha leaned forward, her eyes full of curiosity.

"That thing inside you," said the Tree softly, "is the same thing inside me, as well."

Nisha's eyes widened "Really? That's amazing!"

The Tree nodded. "If you quieten your mind, you can feel it."

Nisha closed her eyes. She began to sense something deep within – a stillness, a glow. Suddenly, she felt everything was connected – the Tree, the flowers, the butterflies, the ants, the sand, the rocks, even the distant stars.

Her face lit up, and she laughed joyfully, her laughter blending with the whisper of the wind

Nisha's eyes sparkled "That's really wonderful, Tree. Thank you. How can I make sure I remember the secret"

"I'll teach you a simple technique," said the Tree kindly. "Can you chant the word AUM?"

Nisha nodded eagerly. "Yes, of course I can! A... U... M..."

Her voice echoed softly through the garden, blending with the rustle of leaves.

Nisha tilted her head curiously. "But how is it connected to the three worlds?"

"Easy," replied the Tree. "The sound A represents the waking world, U represents the dream world, and M represents the deep sleep world."

Nisha grinned "I get it! Easy peasy!"

Then she paused thoughtfully. "Wait… what about the observing thingy? AUM doesn't cover that, does it?"

The Tree's voice softened "Ah, that's a very good question, Nisha. The fourth state cannot be described by sound. It is the silence that follows AUM. When you chant, pause for a moment and listen. That silence… is the presence that observes all the worlds."

Nisha closed her eyes and whispered softly,

"A…U…M…"

The silence after the sound felt alive.

The sunlight glowed through the leaves. Nisha felt a soft warmth spread through her chest.

She looked around – at the flowers, the bees, the stars fading in daylight – and felt something shining inside everything.

"Thank you, tree," she said softly. "Now I know. The changeless one lives in us all."

The tree rustled gently, as if bowing in silence.

Story based on the hindu scripture

Mandukya Upanishad

Mandukya means Frog in Sanskrit language

Once we realise the secret of AUM, our happiness will jump to new heights!

www.ingramcontent.com/pod-product-compliance
Lightning Source LLC
Chambersburg PA
CBRC091202070526
44583CB00008B/178